LIVELY LITTLE LOGS

Making Log Cabin Miniatures

Donna Fite McConnell

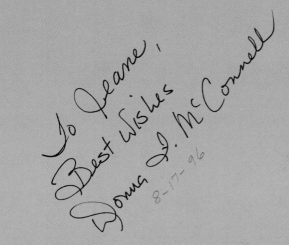

Credits

Editor-in-Chief   Barbara Weiland
Managing Editor   Greg Sharp
Technical Editor   Ursula Reikes
Copy Editor   Liz McGehee
Cover Design   Chris Christiansen
Text Design   Judy Petry
Typesetting   Laura Jensen
Photography   Brent Kane
Illustration and Graphics   Laurel Strand

Lively Little Logs©
©1993 by Donna Fite McConnell

That Patchwork Place, Inc., PO Box 118, Bothell, WA 98041-0118 USA

Printed in the United States of America
98 97 96 95   6 5 4

Library of Congress Cataloging-in-Publication Data
Fite McConnell, Donna.
    Lively little logs/Donna Fite McConnell.
        p.   cm.
    ISBN 1–56477–027–3:
    1. Patchwork—Patterns.   2. Machine quilting—Patterns.   3. Wall hangings.   I. Title.
    TT835.F573 1993
    746.46—dc20   93–8014
                                                                                                CIP

CONTENTS

Acknowledgments

I wish to thank:

My daughter, Micah, who has been such a help to me in writing this book with her typing, editing, and support;

My husband, Father Gary, who has been my strength when I thought I couldn't go any further;

Chris Lasley, my photographer and friend;

Deon Marion, for coming through at the last minute to help me get models ready for photography;

India, my granddaughter, who helped me run the copy machine;

My friends in the Arkansas Quilters Guild, too many to name, who have had faith in me and elected me as an officer on their board over the past eleven years and elected me guild president for the 1993 term;

And to Nancy Martin and her staff, who invited me to write this book.

Dedication

This book is dedicated to Al and Wanda Fite, my father and mother, without whom I would never have had time to write this book. Their help in sorting, pasting, and stuffing patterns has made my job much easier. And to my husband, Father Gary, whose encouragement and undying support, despite lack of meals, unsewn buttons, and my being away from home much of the time, has kept me on track.

And to India, my granddaughter, who at seven years old, loves to go to quilt shows, can't wait to be old enough to work in my booth, and thinks "Memaw's" quilts are her favorite.

PREFACE

There is something very special about being a quilter. Quilting has a way of tying us to others' lives, and the memories we make while we are quilting stay with us long after a quilt has been completed. A few years ago, a friend and I finished a collaborative quilt. Although we did not work on the quilt together at the same time, we both shared in its progress until it was completed. During that time, many things were going on in each of our lives. The doctor discovered a lump in my breast that resulted in surgery. My friend was recovering from a severe illness with a lengthy convalescence. We each had different things, some wonderful, some stressful, going on in our lives. When we finished our quilt, we entered it in several quilt shows. It won some ribbons and was eventually purchased by the Museum of the American Quilters Society in Paducah, Kentucky. Today, as I sat here at my computer, trying to tie up the loose ends of this book, a catalog from the American Quilters Society came in the mail, and there, on the cover of the catalog, was our quilt. Memories of the time when we both worked on it came flooding back. Even though our lives change and time goes on, memories of times past remain with us, and those memories remind us of friends and the visions and goals we once shared together.

I like writing quotations on some of my quilts, and my favorite one is: "I stitch into my quilts the memories I make with my friends." Whether I am quilting with a group at another person's home or sitting at my sewing machine in my own home, many things, outside of my quilting, are happening in my life. Most of my very best friends are quilters. The times we have shared together make some of my best memories. Many times, when I have picked up a quilt, those memories that were made when I worked on it return to me again.

As you work on the projects in this book, be aware of the world around you. Remember the people in your life who are special to you and the things that have brought joy or maybe even sorrow, but most of all, remember that memories are a very important part of our lives, and the memories you make while quilting will return to you again.

Happy quilting,

Donna F. McConnell

INTRODUCTION

There are many quilt blocks, but none more closely represents the "pattern of perfection" of the American quilt block than the Log Cabin block. Nineteenth-century quilters used scraps of both precious and utilitarian fabrics to create the "logs" that were the foundation of the block. Small bits of red fabric were reserved for the central square that represents the chimney. Log Cabin quilts were made of silks, satins, calicoes, and flour sacks. Antique Log Cabin quilts that have survived the years are testimony to the amazing variations that can be achieved with this simple pattern.

About six years ago, I sat down at my sewing machine in a corner of my dining room determined to make a Log Cabin block. I began with 1¾"-wide strips to make my first block. I was hooked! Then I began experimenting with the block to see just how small I could make these lovely little logs. I have gone from my original 8" block to the 1¾" block I currently use for my projects. Not content to stop there, I have begun incorporating appliqué and other embellishments with my miniature blocks. Along the way, I have developed my quilting career, and the dining room and living room are now located at the back of my house. The original rooms are now my two-room studio. How is that for priorities?! I hope my own miniature variation on the Log Cabin theme will inspire you to continue in the quiltmaking tradition of our grandmothers and create your own Log Cabin masterpieces.

EQUIPMENT AND SUPPLIES

Sewing Machine

A good straight-stitch sewing machine can be used on the quilts and projects that do not include appliqué; however, many of these patterns include machine appliqué. To machine appliqué, you need a machine that can make a zigzag stitch or a stitch similar to a blanket stitch. Play around with your machine until you find a stitch that is pleasing to you. On my machine, I have found a stitch that looks very much like hand appliqué, and when I adjust the length and width to a scant $1/16$", it works very well.

An open-toe embroidery foot, a darning foot, and a walking foot are helpful. The embroidery foot helps you to see where you are stitching while you are appliquéing. The darning foot is necessary when you do free-motion quilting around the appliqué designs, and the walking foot helps keep your work smooth while you are doing straight-stitch machine quilting. (See page 17 for illustrations of these feet.)

Cutting Tools

❧ Sharp fabric scissors. My favorite scissors are 4" embroidery scissors. They never leave my hand when I'm sewing at the machine. I use them not only as scissors but also as a stiletto to guide little edges under the presser foot.

❧ Utility scissors for cutting template plastic and paper-backed fusible webbing.

❧ Rotary cutter, mat, and cutting guides for cutting strips.

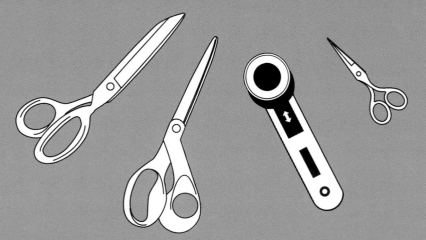

Threads

❧ Cotton or polyester thread for piecing blocks. Use a neutral-colored thread.

❧ Machine embroidery thread for machine appliqué. Match thread to colors of fabric for machine appliqué whenever possible. If you cannot match the fabric exactly, a darker shade looks better than a lighter one.

❧ Monofilament or nylon invisible thread for machine quilting. Use the smoke color on dark fabrics and the clear on light fabrics.

❧ Metallic threads for quilting and decorative stitching. I use metallic threads a lot. The "sparkle" seems to enhance the tiny logs. If you have problems with metallic threads fraying in your machine, your needle may be too small; try a larger needle. I normally use an 80/12.

Fabrics

I use 100% cotton fabrics. I have found that polyester and cotton/poly blends do not work well at all with these narrow strips. When pressed with a hot iron, they have a tendency to shrink, which can then distort your entire block. Cotton fabrics with metallic finishes add a wonderful sparkle and liven up your projects.

I generally do not wash my fabrics first when making decorative quilts. Most likely, they will not be washed later. If you are going to be using a marking pen or pencil for quilting lines, by all means, wash the fabric first because you will have to wash out the markings when you are finished. If you use dark solids like reds, test a small piece in hot water to check for bleeding. If a noticeable amount of dye is released into the water, then wash the fabric before using it. Check for bleeding again, and if the fabric continues to bleed, select another fabric.

Color

Color is a matter of personal choice. I always seem to gravitate toward darker fabrics. It is difficult for me to remember to buy light fabrics, but they are essential in Log Cabin blocks.

Since Log Cabin blocks are high-contrast blocks of light and dark fabrics, I recommend choosing at least six light and six dark fabrics. Remember, the more fabrics you use, the more interesting your piece will be. Try to choose definite lights and definite darks. If it is hard for you to decide if a fabric is light or dark, discard it.

Be careful when using large-print fabrics, since several areas within one fabric may appear to be different fabrics when strips are cut. Sometimes, I choose a fabric that has a nice background for the light side but then have to discard some of it because the fabric has dark areas that will cause a strip to look dark when placed on the light side. To add interest, I like to use large floral prints in the borders. The rule has always been: "For small quilts, use small prints." Try breaking this rule. You will be happy with the results.

Other Supplies

- Iron and ironing board or mat next to your sewing machine
- Tear-away stabilizer, such as Pellon Stitch and Tear™
- Hand-sewing needles
- Straight pins
- Thimble
- Template plastic
- Paper-backed fusible web, such as Wonder-Under™
- Lightweight batting
- Fine-line permanent marking pen in brown or black

BASIC INSTRUCTIONS

Rotary-Cutting Techniques

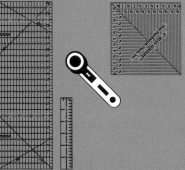

Rotary cutting is a fast and easy method for cutting the strips for Log Cabin blocks. All you need is a rotary cutter, a rotary-cutting mat, and a clear acrylic ruler.

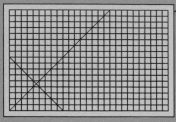

Rotary cutters are available in different sizes and different handle shapes. Choose one that is comfortable for you. Rotary mats also come in many sizes, some with marked grids and some without. The larger mats are useful when cutting full widths of fabric, and the smaller mats are handy to have next to the sewing machine when cutting blocks apart.

Any of the longer rulers—12", 18", or 24"—are ideal for cutting strips. A small 1" x 6" ruler is handy for cutting blocks apart. A square ruler, either 4" x 4" or 6" x 6", is especially helpful for squaring up the blocks.

If you have never used a rotary cutter before, carefully follow the manufacturer's safety precautions.

1. If you are cutting strips from 44"-wide fabric, make another fold from center fold to selvage edge so you are cutting through four layers of fabric. Position the fabric on the cutting mat with the fold toward you, the raw edges to the left, and the remainder of the fabric on the right. You can rotary cut strips from any length of fabric. These small blocks are a good way to use up scraps, so the length of the strips doesn't matter.

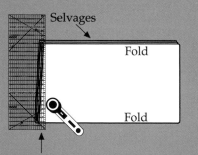

Selvages

Fold

Fold

Trim this
edge away.

2. Align the straight edge of a clear acrylic ruler over the raw edge, along the straight grain of the fabric. Hold the ruler firmly in place with your left hand. (Reverse if you are left-handed.) Roll the rotary cutter along the edge of the ruler across the fabric, always remembering to roll the cutter away from you. Discard this first strip.

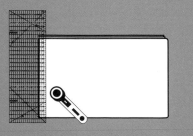

3. Measure ¾" inch from the fabric edge and align the ¾" line on the ruler with the cut edge of the fabric. Cut the fabric into ¾"-wide strips.

4. After every two or three cuts, check to see that the cut edge is still on the straight grain of the fabric. Because fabric has a tendency to shift very slightly while cutting, I "true up" the edge after several cuts. Find the straight grain of the fabric again and make a cut to straighten the edge before cutting the remainder of your strips.

Cutting Strips for Log Cabin Blocks

Since I make so many Log Cabin blocks, I always cut two or three ¾"-wide strips whenever I get new fabric and segregate the strips according to lights and darks. Then whenever I get ready to make a project, I don't have to stop and cut strips for my blocks. I recommend making a practice block before starting a project. All dimensions for cutting include a ¼"-wide seam allowance.

Piecing the Log Cabin Blocks

All of the projects in this book are made with the traditional Log Cabin block, using ¾"-wide strips. Although some projects have blocks that contain all light fabrics and some that contain all dark fabrics, they are all constructed in the same manner. Rows or "logs" are added in numerical order as shown at right.

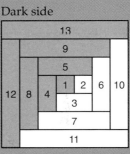

Dark side

Light side

Use the quick-piecing or chain-piecing technique to piece Log Cabin blocks. Be sure your machine is clean and well oiled and your needle is sharp. You should change your needle after every 10–12 hours of sewing time. Most of us do not do this, but it does make a difference. Use a stitch length of 12 to 14 stitches per inch. It is not necessary to backstitch at the beginning and end of a seam, since the next row of stitching will cross over previous rows and secure the threads.

Because sewing machines and seam allowances vary, there may be a slight variation between your blocks and another person's blocks. Your Log Cabin blocks should all be the same size, 2¼", including seam allowances. To help you keep a consistent ¼"-wide seam, try a magnetic seam guide on your machine; however, do not use it on a computerized machine. You can also use adhesive seam guides, which are commercially available; several layers of masking tape; or a strip of moleskin, available at drugstores.

1. The center of the block (the chimney) and the first log are the same size. To quick piece this unit, place a dark strip (Log #1, which is traditionally red) and a light strip together (Log #2) with right sides facing and raw edges even. Sew the strips together along one edge, using a ¼"-wide seam allowance.

2. Press the seam toward Log #2.

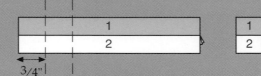

3. Using a rotary cutter and ruler, cut the sewn strips into ¾"-wide units. Cut as many units as you need for your project. Sometimes, I make a few extra blocks in case I have any problems squaring up some of them. These extra blocks can usually be salvaged and can be used for ornaments, key chains, or other smaller projects.

4. Choose a second light strip (Log #3) and lay this strip on the machine, right side up. Place each small unit (Logs #1 and #2), right side down, on top of the strip, as close together as possible without overlapping them. Stitch each block in place as shown. Log #2 should be closest to you as you stitch the blocks to the second light strip.

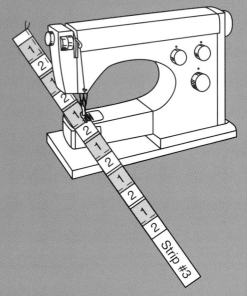

5. Press the seam toward Log #3, the newest log, then cut the blocks apart, using a rotary cutter and ruler.

6. Place a dark strip, Log #4, face up on the machine. Place the blocks, right side down, on top of the strip, as close together as possible without overlapping them. Log #3, the newest log, should be closest to you. Sew each block onto the strip as shown.

7. Press the seams toward Log #4, the newest log; then cut the blocks apart, using a rotary cutter and ruler.

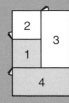

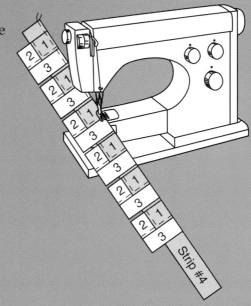

8. Continue adding logs around the block, alternating two light strips and two dark strips until you have three complete rows around the "chimney." Your block should measure 2¼", including seam allowances.

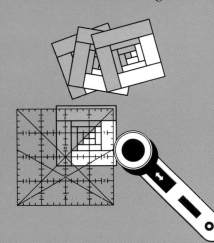

Machine Appliqué

Machine appliqué has become easier and faster since the advent of paper-backed fusible web, such as Wonder-Under. Intricate designs can be ironed to a background and appliquéd with a very small zigzag stitch in no time at all.

Tip

After you have added one complete row of logs around the chimney, check your block to make sure it is still square. The block should measure 1¼" x 1¼", including seam allowances. If necessary, use a small 4" x 4" or 6" x 6" square ruler to trim the edges ever so slightly, to square up the block.

Check your block again after the second row of logs have been added and trim if necessary. The block should measure 1¾" x 1¾", including seam allowances.

Check the final measurement of the block after all logs have been added and trim if necessary. The completed block should measure 2¼" x 2¼", including seam allowances.

It is very important when squaring up the block to trim the edges from all four sides; otherwise, the block will be lopsided.

Preparing Appliqué Pieces

Choose one of the following two methods to prepare pieces for machine appliqué.

Method 1—Making Plastic Templates

This method works especially well for me because I have developed a library of fabrics that I have already prepared for appliqué. I use these appliqué fabrics for flowers, birds, leaves, and bows. I buy fat quarters anytime I see a fabric that would work well in one of my designs. The first thing I do is iron paper-backed fusible web to the back of the fabric. Then, when I want to cut a shape from the fabric, I simply trace around the appropriate plastic template and cut it out. I don't need to spend time ironing the paper-backed fusible web to various bits and pieces of fabric.

1. Iron paper-backed fusible web to wrong side of fabric.

2. Make plastic templates of the pattern pieces for the appliqué design.

3. Trace the pieces onto the paper-backed side of appropriate fabrics, remembering to reverse pieces as indicated if necessary.

4. Cut out the pieces on the drawn line; seam allowances are not necessary in machine appliqué.

5. Remove the paper backing and arrange the appliqué design on your background as shown in the quilt plan.

6. Press pieces with a hot iron to fuse into place.

Method 2—Tracing on Paper-Backed Fusible Web

In this method, the pattern pieces are traced onto the paper side of paper-backed fusible web before the fusible web is ironed to the fabric. This method eliminates the need for plastic templates.

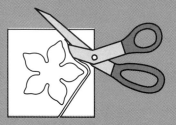

1. With the paper side up, place the paper-backed fusible web on top of the appliqué pattern pieces to be traced.

2. Trace the shapes on the paper side of the fusible web.

3. Cut each of the shapes from the paper-backed fusible web slightly larger than the actual shape. This is *not* a seam allowance.

4. Place the paper-backed fusible web, with the drawn shape, onto the wrong side of the appropriate fabric, web side down. Press in place with a hot iron.

5. Cut out the shape from the fabric on the drawn line; seam allowances are not necessary in machine appliqué.

6. Remove the paper backing.

7. Arrange the appliqué design on your background as shown in the quilt plan. Then press the pieces with a hot iron to fuse into place.

Appliquéing the Pieces

Use a piece of tear-away stabilizer behind your work to keep your appliqué nice and flat. Hold it in place with your fingers until you start stitching; then your stitches will hold it in place.

Thread through extra eye.

Set your machine for a tiny, satin zigzag stitch. Use an open-toe embroidery foot and thread to match the color of your appliqué fabric. If you have never machine appliquéd before, practice on some scrap pieces before working on your actual design. The tension should be slightly looser on the top thread so that the bobbin thread does not pull up to the top and show on the right side of your work. Some machines have a small eye on the bobbin case that can be threaded to add extra tension, which will keep the bobbin thread from showing. If you cannot adjust your tension, use the same color thread in your bobbin as you use on the top.

Position the appliqué under the needle so that you are always stitching toward yourself. Stitch over the raw edges of the design so that the outside edge of the stitching actually goes into the background fabric, and the inside edge of the stitching goes into the design about $\frac{1}{16}$".

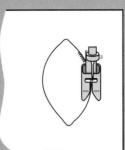

Work slowly up to the points. If you can adjust the width of your zigzag stitch easily, decrease the stitch width before and after a point; then increase the stitch width back to normal. This adjustment will get easier with practice. When stitching around a curve, lift the presser foot, keeping the needle in the down position to hold the fabric in place, and turn the piece slightly before beginning to stitch again. Work slowly to keep your work neat.

Change the top thread each time you move to a different color of fabric. There is no need to re-thread your bobbin each time if the bobbin thread does not show.

Continue until all pieces have been appliquéd. Be sure all of the raw edges of the appliqué are covered. Remove the tear-away stabilizer from the back. Press your work so that it lies flat.

Writing with a Permanent Pen

To add line-drawing embellishments to your work, use a permanent pen. I find that an 03 pen is a little easier to write with than an 01. The brands that seem to be the most permanent are Pilot SC-UF, Pigma, and Niji Stylist II. The Stylist II has a nice, rich brown, which is my favorite for the stems and tendrils. It is a little harder to control than the Pilot because the ink seems to be wetter, but Pilot no longer makes a brown.

Be sure to use a stabilizer behind your fabric. Freezer paper works well when ironed onto the back. The shiny side of the freezer paper is a wax finish that will not harm fabric when it is pulled away. If you are drawing stems and tendrils after appliquéing borders, be sure to do this before you remove the tear-away stabilizer.

Practice on some scraps before writing on your actual project. Sometimes, changing the angle of the pen will keep the point from grabbing at the weave. Soon you will feel comfortable with the pen traveling over the weave.

When drawing tendrils, use a circular motion that involves your whole arm, not just your wrist. You will get a much more natural swirl. Practice, practice, practice! It's really fun once you get the hang of it.

Adding Borders

All of the projects in this book use straight-cut borders. I have not included specific measurements for cutting the length of the borders. Because of slight variations in individual seam allowances and the small size of these quilts, the measurements of your finished quilt top may vary slightly from mine.

1. Measure the length of the quilt top at the center from raw edge to raw edge. Cut two border strips to that measurement and mark the centers of the border strips and the sides of the quilt top.

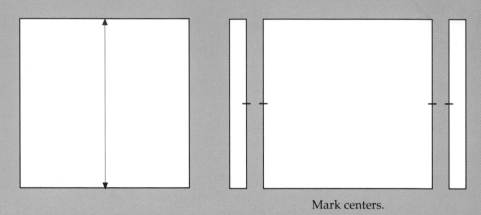

Mark centers.

Sew the border strips to the sides of the quilt, matching ends and centers and easing as necessary.

Tip

If you have to do any easing, it's helpful to pin border strips to the quilt top.

2. Measure the width of the quilt top at the center from raw edge to raw edge, including the border strips you just added to the sides. Cut two border strips to that measurement and mark the centers of the border strips and the top and bottom of the quilt top. Sew the border strips to the top and bottom of the quilt, matching ends and centers and easing as necessary.

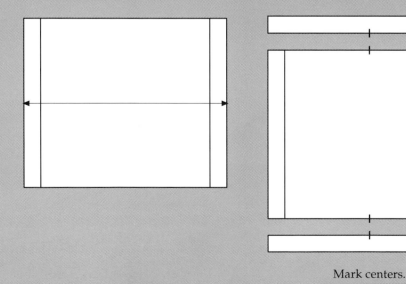

Mark centers.

Finishing the Quilt

I like thin quilts, so I normally split Mountain Mist Quilt Light Batting in half. (Because it is bonded, it will pull apart easily.) Or, you can use Hobbs Thermore Batting.

Cut a piece of batting and a piece of backing fabric 1½" to 2" larger than the quilt top on all sides. Press backing fabric if necessary. Lay backing, wrong side up, on table or work surface. Place batting on top of backing. Place quilt top, right side up, on top of batting to make a quilt "sandwich." Smooth out any wrinkles and pin layers together if necessary. Basting is normally not necessary on these small projects. Most of the time, you can pin baste with three or four pins to hold the layers together.

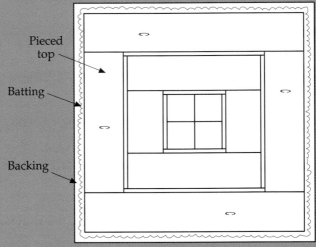

Pieced top

Batting

Backing

Use safety pins to baste layers together for machine quilting.

Machine Quilting

Machine quilting requires a little practice but is well worth the effort. I recommend a walking foot or open-toe embroidery foot (the same foot used for appliquéing) for straight-stitch machine quilting.

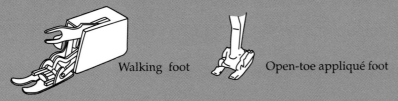

Walking foot   Open-toe appliqué foot

Use monofilament nylon thread on the top and thread to match the backing fabric in the bobbin. Always work from the center outward when quilting. See individual projects for more specific quilting instructions.

To do free-motion quilting, use a darning foot on your machine. Lower the feed dog on the machine or cover it so you have complete control over where the needle goes. You will be hand guiding your quilting stitch. Begin quilting by pushing the fabric with your hands in the direction you want the needle to go. I do not use a hoop. Keep the fabric as flat as possible while working. To keep the threads from snarling underneath, bring the bobbin thread to the top before beginning to stitch by making a single stitch, then pulling on the top thread until the bobbin thread comes through.

Darning foot

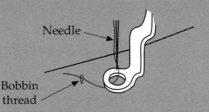

Needle

Bobbin thread

Pulling up bobbin thread

Secure the ends of the thread by making a few stitches in place. Then quilt away a few stitches and snip off beginning threads. Do not turn the quilt while you are working; just move the quilt in the direction you want the stitches to go. You can move up and down, sideways, or in any direction. Watch your fingers; I ran a needle through my finger once, and it was quite painful.

Quilting Suggestions

All the wall hangings are quilted in a similar manner. You can follow my suggestions or create your own quilt designs. The Log Cabin Heart with Floral Appliqué is used as an example to show how each of the areas in the quilt is quilted. Remember, always quilt from the center out toward the edges.

1. Quilt diagonally through and around Log Cabin blocks to emphasize the design, such as the heart. For quilts made with only 4 Log Cabin blocks, quilt diagonally through the center of the blocks.

2. If the quilt includes an appliquéd design, free-motion quilt around the appliquéd pieces in a continuous line so you don't have to stop and restart between pieces. To get from one point to another, you may have to stitch over some previously quilted areas. That's OK as long as you follow the lines exactly.

3. Quilt in-the-ditch on each side of the narrow black borders.

4. Finish by adding one last row of quilting in the outer border, ½"
   from the last narrow black border.

The Log Cabin block shown below is an example of how to quilt
blocks used in the accessories. Use a decorative metallic thread to add
sparkle to your blocks.

Making a Sleeve

Quilts that will be displayed on walls should have a sleeve, attached
to the back at the top edge, to hold a hanging rod.

1. Cut a 6"-wide strip of fabric 1" shorter than the width of the quilt.
   Fold the short ends ¼" to the wrong side and press. Fold the edge ¼"
   again and stitch.

2. Fold the fabric in half lengthwise, matching wrong sides and raw
   edges, and press.

3. Center and pin the sleeve on the back, matching the raw edges of the
   sleeve with the raw edges at the top edge of the quilt. Do not sew the
   sleeve in place until the binding has been added; then blindstitch the
   bottom fold of the sleeve to the back.

Binding

I prefer to use straight-grain binding on all of my quilts.

1. Cut 1¾"-wide strips across the width of the fabric. Make enough binding to go around the perimeter of the quilt, plus 2"–3".

2. If you have to piece the binding strip, seam the ends at a 45° angle to make a long, continuous strip; press seams open.

Fold the strip in half lengthwise, wrong sides together, and press. Unfold one end of the binding and turn under ¼" at a 45° angle to create a finished edge at the end of the binding and distribute the bulk so you won't have a lump where the two ends of the binding come together.

3. Starting in the middle at the bottom edge of your quilt, lay the binding strip on the front of the quilt, lining up the raw edges of the binding with the raw edges of the quilt. Begin stitching about 1" from the beginning of the binding, using a ¼"-wide seam allowance. When you reach the corner, stop stitching ¼" from the edge of the quilt and backstitch.

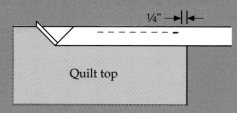

4. Turn the quilt to sew along the next edge. Fold the binding up and away from the quilt.

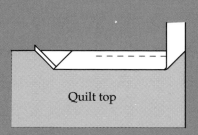

5. Fold the binding again to bring it along the edge of the quilt. There will be a 45° fold at the corner; the straight fold should be even with the top edge of the quilt. Put the needle back down ¼" from the top edge and continue stitching to the next corner.

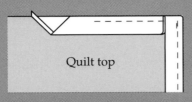

Repeat at each corner until you are about 1" from where you began. Trim off the binding, leaving about a 1" overlap. Fold the raw edge back and insert the beginning of the binding into the fold at the starting point and finish stitching.

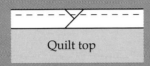

6. Trim away excess backing and batting.

7. Fold the binding to the back; the folded edge of the binding should just cover the machine-stitching line. Blindstitch the binding in place.

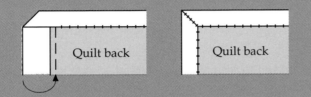

Making Prairie Points

Some wall hangings in this book have been finished with a prairie-point edging instead of a binding. I like to cut the squares for prairie points from all of the fabrics I used in my quilt instead of from a single fabric. Check the individual projects for the required number of squares. Prairie points are stitched to the right side of the quilt. Be sure to leave about 2" of the border unquilted near the edge.

1. Cut squares, 1½" x 1½". Fold the squares in half diagonally, then in half diagonally again.

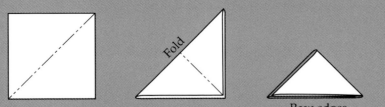

2. Fold the batting and backing out of the way and secure with straight pins while you stitch the prairie points into place.

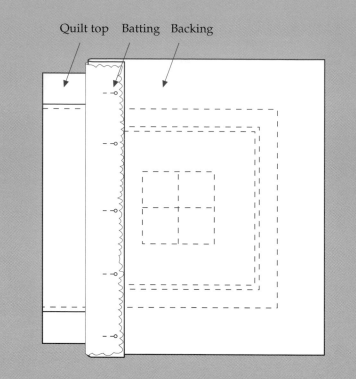

Quilt top   Batting   Backing

3. Working on the right side of the quilt top, place a folded triangle ½" from the corner on one of the sides, matching raw edges as shown. Stitch the prairie point about half way. Stop with the needle in the down position to hold the prairie point in place.

4. Pick up another prairie point and slip it about ¼" into the fold of the first prairie point; stitch about half way.

5. Continue adding prairie points and stitching, choosing colors at random, until you reach the other corner. You may have to adjust the last few points to get them to fit. Keep the last prairie point about ½" from the corner of the quilt so you can press the prairie points back without having to fold any portion of the triangle under.

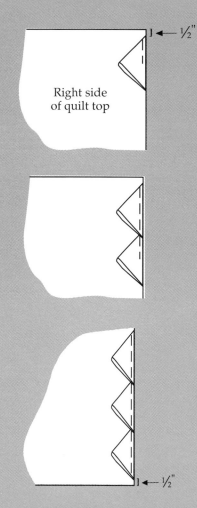

Right side of quilt top

½"

6. Press the prairie points toward the outside edges of the quilt.

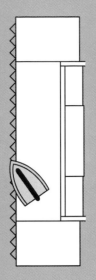

Turn the quilt over and smooth the batting flat against the front. Trim away excess batting so the edge of the batting butts up to the raw edge of the pressed-open prairie points.

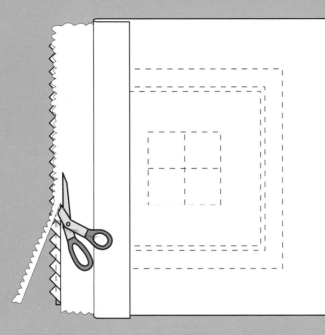

7. Trim the backing if necessary, leaving about ½" to turn under. Fold the edges of the backing to cover the seams and pin in place. Do this on both sides and bottom of quilt. Check from the front side to see if any of the backing shows between the points. Blindstitch the backing in place on these three sides, making sure the stitches do not go through to the front of the quilt.

Attach a sleeve to the top of the quilt. Follow the directions for making the sleeve on page 19 through step 2.

Center and pin the sleeve to the top of the back only, matching raw edges of the sleeve with the raw edges of the backing. Machine stitch the sleeve to the backing, using a ¼"-wide seam allowance.

Raw edges

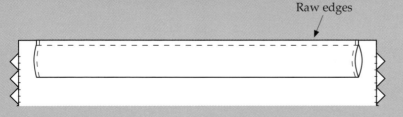

Turn under the stitched edge and pin in place. Blindstitch to finish.

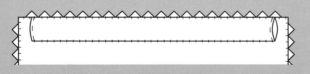

Signing Your Quilt!

It is very important to sign your work. After all, you want your grandchildren to know exactly who made that family heirloom! Here is one way to sign your quilt.

1. Make a plastic template of one of the heart patterns below.
2. Iron a piece of freezer paper to the wrong side of a 4" square of muslin.
3. Trace the heart shape onto the freezer paper.
4. Cut out the heart, adding a ¼"-wide seam allowance for turning under the edges.
5. Draw one of the label designs below onto the right side of the muslin. Use a permanent fine-line brown or black pen.
6. Write your name and date in the center of the heart.
7. Remove the freezer paper and pin the heart on the back of the quilt.
8. Appliqué the heart in place.

Lively Little Log Heart
by Donna McConnell, Searcy,
Arkansas, 1990, 17½" x 17½".
The combination of light and
dark fabrics in the thirty-six
blocks gives life to this simple
miniature quilt.

Fifty-six-Block Little Log Heart
by Donna McConnell, Searcy,
Arkansas, 1991, 23½" x 21¾".

Searcy Star 1 & 2
by Donna McConnell, Searcy, Arkansas, 1991, 24½" x 24½". When Donna designed this little quilt, she named it in honor of her hometown.

Lively Little Log Cabins and Appliqué Hearts *by Donna McConnell, Searcy, Arkansas, 1990, 16" x 18½". This quilt was featured in* Mini Quilts *by Anita Murphy and her friends.*

Circle of Flowers and Ribbon Wreath *by Donna McConnell, Searcy, Arkansas, 1990, 14½" x 14½". These two little quilts were Donna's first designs in which she combined machine appliqué with her little logs.*

Bluebirds and Flowers Around Little Logs *by Deon Marion, Searcy, Arkansas, 1991, 14½" x 14½". The bluebirds and flowers encircle the little logs in this quilt.*

Floral Heart Wreath with Log Cabins *by Deon Marion, Searcy, Arkansas, 1992, 16" x 16". This quilt would make a nice wedding present.*

Log Cabin Heart with Floral Appliqué Border *by Donna McConnell, Searcy, Arkansas, 1991, 23" x 23". The heart in this quilt has been accented with a floral border and finished with Prairie Points.*

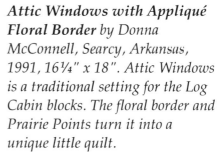

Attic Windows with Appliqué Floral Border *by Donna McConnell, Searcy, Arkansas, 1991, 16¼" x 18". Attic Windows is a traditional setting for the Log Cabin blocks. The floral border and Prairie Points turn it into a unique little quilt.*

Santas in the Forest *by Donna McConnell, Searcy, Arkansas, 1991, 18½" x 21". This little Christmas quilt with its holly border is one of Donna's favorite designs.*

Lively Barn Raising
*by Donna McConnell, Searcy,
Arkansas, 1993, 20½" x 20½".*

Large and Small Pincushions
*by Donna McConnell, Searcy,
Arkansas, 1992, 3½" x 3½" and
1¾" x 1¾".*

Ornaments and Key Chains
*by Donna McConnell, Searcy,
Arkansas, 1992, 2¼" x 2¼".
Make a darling little Christmas
tree covered with these little
ornaments. The key chains are
a quick and simple gift project
that requires only a small
investment of time and fabric.*

Checkbook Cover *by Donna McConnell, Searcy, Arkansas, 1992, 4" x 7¾". Keep those accounts in order with a quilted cover.*

Needle Case *by Donna McConnell, Searcy, Arkansas, 1992, 4¼" x 4¼". These useful little projects make wonderful gifts for your quilting and needleworking friends.*

Eyeglass Case *by Donna McConnell, Searcy, Arkansas, 1992, 3" x 6½".*

Chatelaine
by Donna McConnell, Searcy, Arkansas, 1992, 3¾" x 4¼". Use the chatelaine to keep up with your scissors, needles, and thread while quilting.

Name Tags
by Donna McConnell, Searcy, Arkansas, 1992, 4" x 4". Do you need a name tag at your quilt-guild meeting? This little name tag will bring you lots of comments.

ABOUT THE PROJECTS

The patterns and instructions for the projects in this book are divided into two sections. The first is devoted to wall hangings; the second contains accessory items that you can make in a short amount of time for wonderful gifts. All of the projects use the basic Log Cabin block. Please read carefully the Basic Instructions, beginning on page 10, before starting the projects.

Remember that since these are small projects, they are a great way to use up scraps (especially for the blocks and the appliqué pieces). I have not given specific color guidelines for the projects other than to call for light or dark fabrics or solids when they are used specifically.

If selecting colors is a problem for you, try this method. Choose a theme fabric that you like. Then pick out fabrics that contain the colors used in your theme fabric. You know the colors will go together if they are used in the same fabric. You may or may not use the theme fabric in your final project, but using this method assures you of colors that will blend together.

The yardage requirements for all projects are ample. Many times, I have suggested ⅛ yard even though it may not take quite that much. You may find that many fabric shops will not cut less than ¼-yard pieces; you are very lucky if you can get them to cut ⅛ yard. If you do not have scraps on hand, a fat quarter works very well and I buy lots of them. It is the easiest way to increase your fabric "palette" without having a big investment of fabric on your shelves.

Template patterns for the appliquéd designs are included with individual projects. Appliqué templates do not include a seam allowance since it is not necessary for machine appliqué. If you choose to hand appliqué any of these projects, be sure to add a ⅛"- or ¼"-wide seam allowance all around for turning under the edges.

All borders are straight cut, not mitered. The side borders are always added first, then the top and bottom borders. Some borders are appliquéd before being sewn to the quilt top.

Seam allowances are always ¼" wide when piecing the blocks or adding borders.

These projects are meant to be fun, so by all means, enjoy yourself!

Wall Hangings

With just a small investment of time and fabric, you can make any of these stunning wall hangings. Brighten your home or make one to give to a friend.

LIVELY LITTLE LOG HEART

Color Photo: page 25
Quilt Size: 17½" x 17½"
36 Blocks

Quilt Plan

Cutting

Cut all strips across the fabric width (crosswise grain).

From assorted light fabrics*, cut a total of:
   10 strips, each ¾" x 40"

From assorted dark fabrics*, cut a total of:
   10 strips, each ¾" x 40"

From solid color, cut:
   1 strip, ¾" x 40", for center of blocks

From black fabric, cut:
   2 strips, each ¾" x 40", for inner border

From floral print, cut:
   2 strips, each 3½" x 40", for outer border
   2 strips, each 1¾" x 40", for binding

From backing fabric, cut:
   1 square, 19" x 19", for backing
   1 rectangle, 6" x 16½", for sleeve

From lightweight batting, cut:
   1 square, 19" x 19"

*If using scraps or fat quarters for the light and dark sides of the blocks, cut enough strip lengths of light and dark fabrics to total the required number of strips shown above.

Directions

1. Follow the Basic Instructions for "Piecing the Log Cabin Blocks" on pages 11–13. Make 36 blocks as shown.

  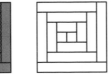

Make 18.   Make 6.   Make 12.

MATERIALS
44"-WIDE FABRIC

Use as many fabrics as possible in the colors of your choice for traditional Log Cabin blocks.

⅛ yd. each of 6 to 8 lights and 6 to 8 darks

⅛ yd. solid color (red is traditional) for center of blocks

⅛ yd. black for inner border

⅛ yd. floral print for outer border and binding

⅝ yd. for backing and sleeve

⅝ yd. lightweight batting

Note: Scraps of light and dark fabrics or fat quarters may also be used for the Log Cabin blocks.

2. Arrange the blocks to form a heart as shown in the quilt plan on page 34. Sew the blocks together in horizontal rows. Press the seams of alternating rows in opposite directions.

3. Sew the rows together, making sure to match the seams between each block.

4. To add inner border, measure the quilt through the center for the correct side border length as shown on page 16. Cut 2 black border strips to the correct length and sew to opposite sides of the quilt top. Measure the width of the quilt through the center, including the side borders. Cut remaining black border strips to the correct length and sew to the top and bottom edges of the quilt top.

5. Measure and add outer borders as described in step 4 above.

6. Layer the quilt with batting and backing; pin baste, using safety pins.

7. Quilt around the Log Cabin heart design and in-the-ditch around borders. Add one row of quilting in the outer border, ½" from the inner border. See page 18.

8. Attach the sleeve and bind the edges of the quilt. See pages 19–21.

FIFTY-SIX-BLOCK LITTLE LOG HEART

Color Photo: page 25
Quilt Size: 23½" x 21¾"
56 Blocks

Quilt Plan

MATERIALS
44"-WIDE FABRIC

Use as many fabrics as possible in the colors of your choice for traditional Log Cabin blocks.

⅛ yd. each of 8 to 10 lights and 8 to 10 darks

⅛ yd. solid color for center of blocks

⅛ yd. black for 1st and 3rd borders

⅛ yd. contrasting fabric for 2nd border

¾ yd. floral print for outer border and binding

1 yd. for backing and sleeve

¾ yd. lightweight batting

Note: Scraps of light and dark fabrics or fat quarters may also be used for the Log Cabin blocks.

Cutting

Cut all strips across the fabric width (crosswise grain).

From assorted light fabrics*, cut a total of:
25 strips, each ¾" x 40"

From assorted dark fabrics*, cut a total of:
10 strips, each ¾" x 40"

From solid color, cut:
2 strips, each ¾" x 40", for center of blocks

From black fabric, cut:
4 strips, each ¾" x 40", for 1st and 3rd borders

From contrasting border fabric, cut:
2 strips, each 1½" x 40", for 2nd border

From floral print, cut:
3 strips, each 3½" x 40", for outer border
3 strips, each 1¾" x 40", for binding

From backing fabric, cut:
1 rectangle, 23" x 25", for backing
1 rectangle, 6" x 21", for sleeve

From lightweight batting, cut:
1 rectangle, 23" x 25"

*If using scraps or fat quarters for the light and dark sides of the blocks, cut enough strip lengths of light and dark fabrics to total the required number of strips shown above.

Directions

1. Follow the Basic Instructions for "Piecing the Log Cabin Blocks" on pages 11–13. Make 56 blocks as shown.

Make 16.

Make 4.

Make 36.

2. Arrange the blocks to form a heart as shown in the quilt plan on page 37. Sew blocks together in horizontal rows. Press seams of alternating rows in opposite directions.

3. Sew the rows together, making sure to match the seams between each block.

4. To add the first border, measure the quilt through the center for the correct side border length as shown on page 16. Cut 2 black border strips to the correct length and sew to opposite sides of the quilt top. Measure the width of the quilt through the center, including the side borders. Cut 2 black border strips to the correct length and sew to the top and bottom edges of the quilt top.

5. Measure and add the second, third, and outer borders as described in step 4.

6. Layer the quilt with batting and backing; pin baste, using safety pins.

7. Quilt around the heart design and in-the-ditch around all of the borders. Add one row of quilting in the outer border, ½" from the third border. See page 18.

8. Attach the sleeve and bind the edges of the quilt. See pages 19–21.

Color Photo: page 26
Quilt Size: 24½" x 24½"
64 Blocks

SEARCY STAR

Quilt Plan

Cutting

Cut all strips across the fabric width (crosswise grain).

From assorted light fabrics*, cut a total of:
18 strips, each ¾" x 40"

From dark fabrics*, cut a total of:
20 strips, each ¾" x 40"

From solid color, cut:
2 strips, each ¾" x 40", for center of blocks

From black fabric, cut:
4 strips, each ¾" x 40", for 1st and 3rd borders

From contrasting fabric, cut:
2 strips, each 1¾" x 40", for 2nd border

From floral print, cut:
3 strips, each 3¾" x 40", for outer border
3 strips, each 1¾" x 40", for binding

From backing fabric, cut:
1 square, 26" x 26", for backing
1 rectangle, 6" x 23", for sleeve

From batting, cut:
1 square, 26" x 26"

*If using scraps or fat quarters for the light and dark sides of the blocks, cut enough strip lengths of light and dark fabrics to total the required number of strips shown above.

Directions

1. Follow the Basic Instructions for "Piecing the Log Cabin Blocks" on pages 11–13. Make 64 blocks as shown.

Make 64.

MATERIALS
44"-WIDE FABRIC

Use as many fabrics as possible in the colors of your choice for traditional Log Cabin blocks.

⅛ yd. each of 6 to 8 lights and 6 to 8 darks

⅛ yd. solid color for center of blocks

⅛ yd. black for 1st and 3rd borders

⅛ yd. contrasting fabric for 2nd border

½ yd. floral print for outer border and binding

1 yd. for backing and sleeve

¾ yd. lightweight batting

Note: Scraps of light and dark fabrics or fat quarters may also be used for the Log Cabin blocks.

2. Arrange the blocks to form a star as shown in the quilt plan on page 40. Sew blocks together in horizontal rows. Press the seams of alternating rows in opposite directions.

3. Sew the rows together, making sure to match the seams between each block.

4. To add the first border, measure the quilt through the center for the correct side border length as shown on page 16. Cut 2 black border strips to the correct length and sew to opposite sides of the quilt top. Measure the width of the quilt through the center, including the side borders. Cut 2 black border strips to the correct length and sew to the top and bottom edges of the quilt top.

5. Measure and add the second, third, and outer borders as described in step 4.

6. Layer the quilt with batting and backing; pin baste, using safety pins.

7. Quilt around the Log Cabin star design, beginning in the center of the quilt, then follow the outline of the diamonds. Quilt in-the-ditch around all of the borders, then add one row of quilting in the outer border, ½" from the third border. See page 18.

8. Attach the sleeve and bind the edges of the quilt. See pages 19–21.

Lively Little Log Cabins and Appliqué Hearts

Color Photo: page 26
Quilt Size: 16" x 18½"
12 Log Cabin Blocks
6 Heart Blocks

Quilt Plan

MATERIALS
44"-WIDE FABRIC

Use as many fabrics as possible in the colors of your choice for traditional Log Cabin blocks.

⅛ yd. each of 6 to 8 lights and 6 to 8 darks

Scrap of solid color for center of blocks

⅛ yd. black for inner border

⅛ yd. contrasting fabric for middle border

⅓ yd. floral print for outer border and binding

⅛ yd. background for heart blocks, side triangles, and corner triangles

Assorted small scraps for hearts, at least 2½" x 2½"

½ yd. for backing and sleeve

½ yd. lightweight batting

Note: Scraps of light and dark fabrics or fat quarters may also be used for the Log Cabin blocks.

Cutting

Cut all strips across the fabric width (crosswise grain).

From assorted light fabrics*, cut a total of:
   6 strips, each ¾" x 20"

From assorted dark fabrics*, cut a total of:
   7 strips, each ¾" x 20"

From solid color, cut:
   1 strip, ¾" x 10", for center of blocks

From black fabric, cut:
   1 strip, ¾" x 40", for inner border

From contrasting fabric, cut:
   2 strips, each 1¾" x 40", for middle border

From floral print, cut:
   2 strips, each 3" x 40", for outer border
   2 strips, each 1¾" x 40", for binding**

From background fabric, cut:
   2 strips, each 2½" x 40", for squares and corner and side triangles

From backing fabric, cut:
   1 rectangle, 18" x 20", for backing
   1 rectangle, 6" x 15", for sleeve

From lightweight batting, cut:
   1 rectangle, 18" x 20"

*If using scraps or fat quarters for the light and dark sides of the blocks, cut enough strip lengths of light and dark fabrics to total the required number of strips shown above.

**Alternate Prairie Point finish: From assorted fabrics used in the quilt, make approximately 64 prairie points.

Directions

1. Follow the Basic Instructions for "Piecing the Log Cabin Blocks" on pages 11–13. Make 12 blocks as shown.

Make 12.

2. Using the template patterns on page 46, make plastic templates for heart, background square, and corner and side triangles.

3. It is important to match the size of the Log Cabin blocks and the background appliqué squares. Compare the completed Log Cabin blocks with the square template. You can either trim the edges of the Log Cabin blocks to match the template, or trim the edges of the template to match the Log Cabin blocks.

4. Using the plastic templates, cut 6 squares, 4 corner triangles, and 10 side triangles from background fabric.

5. Using the method you prefer from pages 13–14 for machine appliqué and the heart of your choice on page 46, either make plastic templates or trace patterns on paper side of fusible web. Cut 6 hearts from assorted fabrics.

6. Follow the Basic Instructions for "Machine Appliqué" on pages 13–15 to appliqué the hearts to the background squares.

7. Arrange the Log Cabin blocks, heart blocks, and triangles as shown. The side triangles and corners are larger than necessary. You will trim them before adding inner border. Sew the blocks into diagonal rows. Press the seams of alternating rows in opposite directions.

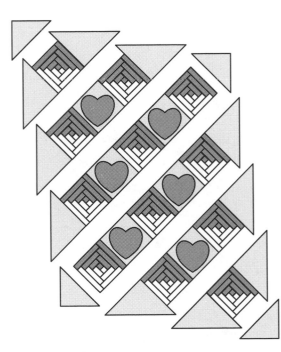

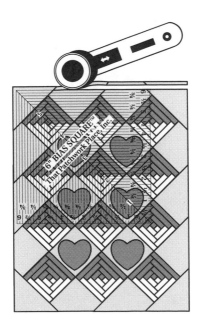

8. Sew the rows together, making sure to match the seams between each block. Add the corner triangles last.

9. Trim sides and square up corners. Using a large square ruler or another similar right-angled ruler, measure ¼" out from the corners of the blocks and trim excess fabric.

10. To add the inner border, measure the quilt through the center for the correct side border length as shown on page 16. Cut 2 black border strips to the correct length and sew to opposite sides of the quilt top. Measure the width of the quilt through the center, including the side borders. Cut the remaining 2 black border strips to the correct length and sew to the top and bottom edges of the quilt top.

11. Measure and add the middle and outer borders as described in step 10.

12. Layer the quilt with batting and backing; pin baste, using safety pins.

13. Free-motion quilt around the hearts. Quilt around the Log Cabin blocks and borders, ending with a row of quilting in the outer border, ½" from the middle border. See page 18.

14. Attach the sleeve and bind the edges of the quilt. See pages 19–21.

15. Alternate finish: Follow the Basic Instructions for "Making Prairie Points" on pages 21–23, using approximately 64 prairie points that have been cut from assorted fabrics used in the quilt; then attach the sleeve to the back of the quilt.

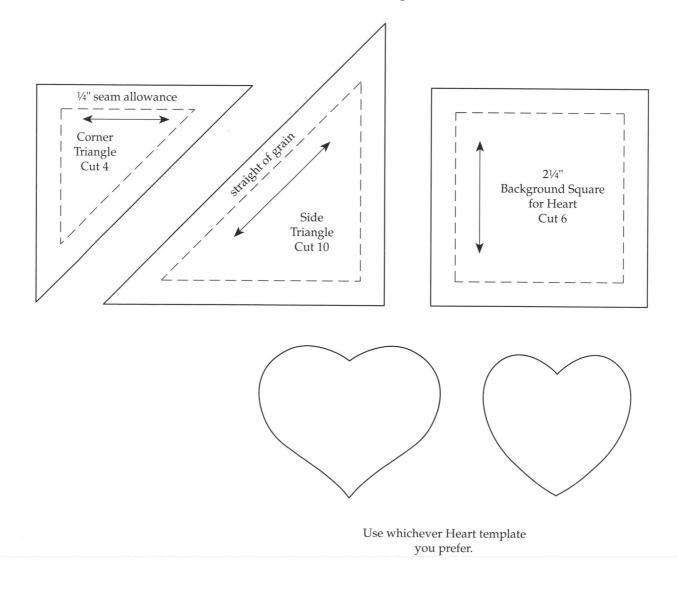

Use whichever Heart template
you prefer.

FLORAL HEART WREATH WITH LOG CABINS

Color Photo: page 28
Quilt Size: 16" x 16"
4 Blocks

Quilt Plan

MATERIALS
44"-WIDE FABRIC

Use as many fabrics as possible in the colors of your choice for traditional Log Cabin blocks.

Scraps or fat quarters of 6 to 8 lights and 6 to 8 darks

Scrap of solid color for center of blocks

⅛ yd. black for 1st and 3rd borders

⅛ yd. background for 2nd border

⅛ yd. contrasting fabric for 4th border

⅓ yd. floral print for outer border and binding

2 different shades of the same color for bow, each 3" x 6"

3 to 5 assorted greens for leaves, each 3" x 4"

6 to 8 assorted colors for flowers, each 3" x 4"

Yellow for flower centers, 3" x 3"

½ yd. for backing and sleeve

½ yd. lightweight batting

Cutting

From assorted light and dark fabrics, cut:
Enough ¾"-wide strips to make 4 Log Cabin blocks

From solid color, cut:
1 strip, ¾" x 3", for center of blocks

From black fabric, cut:
2 strips, each ¾" x 40", for 1st and 3rd borders

From background fabric, cut:
1 strip, 2¾" x 40", for 2nd border

From contrasting fabric, cut:
2 strips, 1¼" x 40", for 4th border

From floral print, cut:
2 strips, each 3" x 40", for outer border
2 strips, each 1¾" x 40", for binding*

From backing fabric, cut:
1 square, 18" x 18", for backing
1 rectangle, 6" x 15", for sleeve

From lightweight batting, cut:
1 square, 18" x 18"

*Alternate Prairie Point finish: From assorted fabrics used in the quilt, make approximately 60 prairie points.

Directions

1. Follow the Basic Instructions for "Piecing the Log Cabin Blocks" on page 11–13. Make 4 blocks as shown.

Make 4.

2. Sew the blocks together as shown.

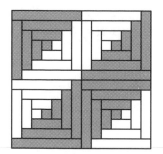

3. To add first border, measure the quilt through the center for the correct side border length as shown on page 16. Cut 2 black border strips to the correct length and sew to opposite sides of the quilt top. Measure the width of the quilt through the center, including the side borders. Cut 2 black border strips to the correct length and sew to the top and bottom edges of the quilt top.

4. Measure and add the second border for the appliquéd flowers, as described in step 3.

5. Using the template patterns at right and below and one of the methods described on pages 13–14, prepare the appliqué pieces.

6. Arrange the bow, flowers, and leaves to form a heart shape as shown in the quilt plan on page 47. Press the design in place with a hot iron. Appliqué the design, following the directions for "Machine Appliqué" on pages 14–15.

7. Before removing the tear-away stabilizer, draw the tendrils for the flowers with a fine-line permanent pen as shown in the quilt plan.

8. Measure and add the third, fourth, and outer borders as described in step 3 above.

9. Layer the quilt with batting and backing; pin baste, using safety pins.

10. Quilt around the Log Cabin blocks. Free-motion quilt around the flowers and leaves. Quilt in-the-ditch around the remaining borders, ending with a row of quilting in the outer border, ½" from the fourth border. See page 18.

11. Attach the sleeve and bind the edges of the quilt. See pages 19–21.

12. Alternate finish: Follow the Basic Instructions for "Making Prairie Points" on pages 21–23, using approximately 60 prairie points that have been cut from assorted fabrics used in the quilt; then attach the sleeve to the back of the quilt.

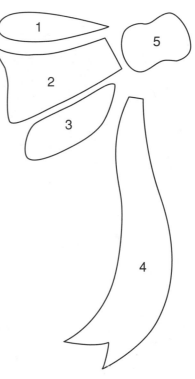

Cut:
1 each of templates 1, 2, 3, 4
   for Bow
1 each of templates 1, 2, 3, 4
   reversed for Bow
1 of template 5 for Bow

Cut:
21 Assorted leaves
4 Tulips
8 Assorted flowers, as shown
   on pattern placement
8 Flower centers

Leaves

Flower center

Tulips

Color Photo: page 27
Quilt Size: 14¹/₂" x 14¹/₂"
4 Blocks

CIRCLE OF FLOWERS

Quilt Plan

Cutting

Cut all strips across the fabric width (crosswise grain).

From assorted light and dark fabrics, cut:
Enough ¾"-wide strips to make 4 Log Cabin blocks

From solid color, cut:
1 strip, ¾" x 3", for center of blocks

From black fabric, cut:
2 strips, each ¾" x 40", for 1st and 3rd borders

From background, cut:
1 strip, 2¾" x 40", for 2nd border

From floral print, cut:
2 strips, each 3" x 40", for outer border
2 strips, each 1¾" x 40", for binding

From backing, cut:
1 square, 16" x 16", for backing
1 rectangle, 6" x 13", for sleeve

From lightweight batting, cut:
1 square, 16" x 16"

Directions

1. Follow the Basic Instructions for "Piecing the Log Cabin Blocks" on pages 11–13. Make 4 blocks as shown.

Make 4.

2. Sew the blocks together as shown.

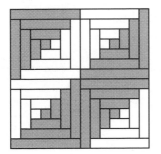

MATERIALS
44"-WIDE FABRIC

Use as many fabrics as possible in the colors of your choice for traditional Log Cabin blocks.

Scraps or fat quarters of 6 to 8 lights and 6 to 8 darks

Scrap of solid color for center of blocks

⅛ yd. black for 1st and 3rd borders

⅛ yd. background for 2nd border

⅓ yd. floral print for outer border and binding

Fabric for bow, 4" x 6"

3 to 4 assorted greens for leaves, each 3" x 3"

4 to 6 assorted colors for flowers, each 3" x 4"

Yellow for flower centers, 3" x 3"

½ yd. for backing and sleeve

½ yd. lightweight batting

3. To add first border, measure the quilt through the center for the correct side border length as shown on page 16. Cut 2 black border strips to the correct length and sew to opposite sides of the quilt top. Measure the width of the quilt through the center, including the side borders. Cut 2 black border strips to the correct length and sew to the top and bottom edges of the quilt top.

4. Measure and add the second border for the appliquéd flowers, as described in step 3.

5. Using the template patterns below and one of the methods described on pages 13–14, prepare the appliqué pieces.

6. Arrange the bow, flowers, and leaves as shown in the quilt plan on page 50. Press the design in place with a hot iron. Appliqué the design, following the directions for "Machine Appliqué" on pages 14–15.

7. Measure and add the third and outer borders as described in step 3 above.

8. Layer the quilt with batting and backing; pin baste, using safety pins.

9. Quilt around the Log Cabin blocks. Free-motion quilt around the flowers and leaves. Quilt in-the-ditch around the remaining borders, ending with a row of quilting in the outer border, ½" from the third border. See page 18.

10. Attach the sleeve and bind the edges of the quilt. See pages 19–21.

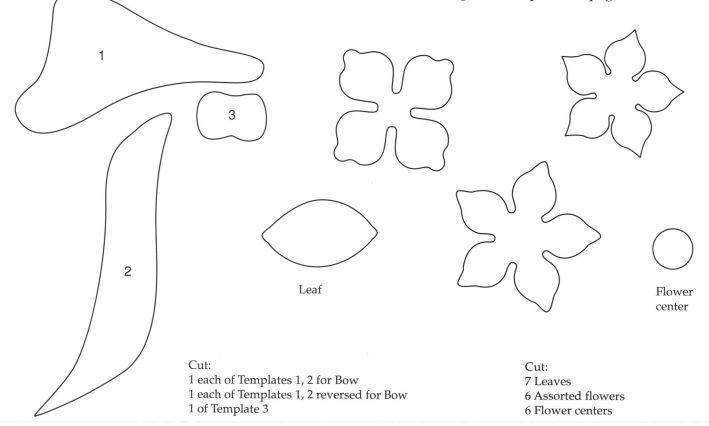

1

3

2

Leaf

Flower center

Cut:
1 each of Templates 1, 2 for Bow
1 each of Templates 1, 2 reversed for Bow
1 of Template 3

Cut:
7 Leaves
6 Assorted flowers
6 Flower centers

RIBBON WREATH

Color photo: page 27
Quilt Size: 14½" x 14½"
4 Blocks

Quilt Plan

MATERIALS
44"-WIDE FABRIC

Use as many fabrics as possible in the colors of your choice for traditional Log Cabin blocks.

Scraps or fat quarters of 6 to 8 lights and 6 to 8 darks

Scrap of solid color for center of blocks

⅛ yd. black for 1st and 3rd borders

⅛ yd. background for 2nd border

⅓ yd. contrasting fabric for outer border and binding

Small scrap of contrasting fabric for bow and wreath

½ yd. for backing and sleeve

½ yd. lightweight batting

Follow the directions for making the Circle of Flowers Wall Hanging on page 50, using the template patterns below. Arrange the design as shown in the quilt plan to make the Ribbon Wreath.

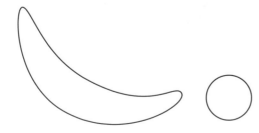

Cut:
6 ribbon shapes
7 circles
See page 52 for template pattern for Bow and cutting instructions.

Color Photo: page 28
Quilt Size: 14½" x 14½"
4 Blocks

BLUEBIRDS AND FLOWERS AROUND LITTLE LOGS

Quilt Plan

Cutting

Cut all strips across the fabric width (crosswise grain).

From assorted light and dark fabrics, cut:
Enough ¾"-wide strips to make 4 Log Cabin blocks

From solid color, cut:
1 strip, ¾" x 3", for center of blocks

From black fabric, cut:
2 strips, each ¾" x 40", for 1st and 3rd borders

From background, cut:
1 strip, 2¾" x 40", for 2nd border

From floral print, cut:
2 strips, each 3" x 40", for outer border
2 strips, each 1¾" x 40", for binding

From backing, cut:
1 square, 16" x 16", for backing
1 rectangle, 6" x 13", for sleeve

From lightweight batting, cut:
1 square, 16" x 16"

Directions

1. Follow the Basic Instructions for "Piecing the Log Cabin Blocks" on pages 11–13. Make 4 blocks as shown.

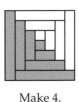

Make 4.

2. Sew the blocks together as shown.

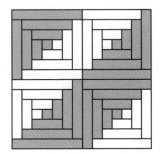

MATERIALS
44"-WIDE FABRIC

Use as many fabrics as possible in the colors of your choice for traditional Log Cabin blocks.

Scraps or fat quarters of 6 to 8 lights and 6 to 8 darks

Scrap of solid color for center of blocks

⅛ yd. black for 1st and 3rd borders

⅛ yd. background for 2nd border

⅓ yd. floral print for outer border

Blue print for birds, 4" x 5"

Darker blue for wings, 1" x 2"

Color of your choice for ribbon, 4" x 6"

Assorted colors for flowers, each 3" x 4"

Yellow for flower centers, 3" x 3"

½ yd. fabric for backing and sleeve

½ yd. lightweight batting

3. To add first border, measure the quilt through the center for the correct side border length as shown on page 16. Cut 2 black border strips to the correct length and sew to opposite sides of the quilt top. Measure the width of the quilt through the center, including the side borders. Cut 2 black border strips to the correct length and sew to the top and bottom edges of the quilt top.

4. Measure and add the second border for the appliquéd birds and flowers as described in step 3.

5. Using the template patterns below and one of the methods described on pages 13–14, prepare the appliqué pieces.

6. Arrange the birds, flowers, and ribbon pieces as shown in the quilt plan on page 54. Press the design in place with a hot iron. Appliqué the design, following the directions for "Machine Appliqué" on pages 14–15.

7. Measure and add the third and outer borders as described in step 3 above.

8. Layer the quilt with batting and backing; pin baste, using safety pins.

9. Quilt around the Log Cabin blocks. Free-motion quilt around the birds, flowers, and ribbon. Quilt in-the-ditch around the remaining borders, ending with a row of quilting in the outer border, ½" from the third border. See page 18.

10. Attach the sleeve and bind the edges of the quilt. See pages 19–21.

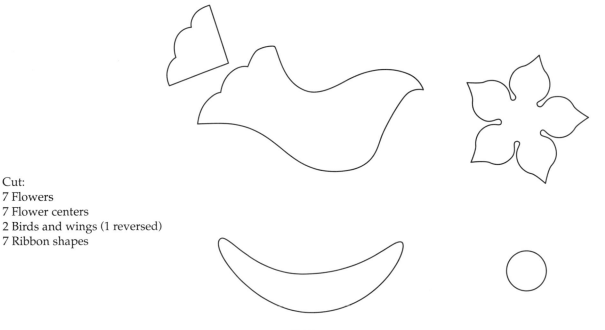

Cut:
7 Flowers
7 Flower centers
2 Birds and wings (1 reversed)
7 Ribbon shapes

Ribbon   Flower center

LOG CABIN HEART WITH FLORAL APPLIQUÉ BORDER

Color Photo: page 28
Quilt Size: 23" x 23"
36 Blocks

Quilt Plan

MATERIALS
44"-WIDE FABRIC

Use as many fabrics as possible in the colors of your choice for traditional Log Cabin blocks.

⅛ yd. each of 8 to 10 lights and 8 to 10 darks

⅛ yd. solid color for center of blocks

⅛ yd. black for 1st and 3rd borders

⅛ yd. background for 2nd border

½ yd. floral print for outer border

10 to 12 assorted colors for hearts and flowers, each 3" x 6"

4 to 6 assorted greens for leaves, each 3" x 6"

Dark brown for stems, 2" x 15"

1 yd. for backing and sleeve

¾ yd. lightweight batting

Note: Scraps of light and dark fabrics or fat quarters may also be used for the Log Cabin blocks.

Cutting

Cut all strips across the fabric width (crosswise grain).

From assorted light fabrics*, cut a total of:
10 strips, each ¾" x 40"

From assorted dark fabrics*, cut a total of:
12 strips, each ¾" x 40"

From solid color, cut:
1 strip, ¾" x 40", for center of blocks

From black fabric, cut:
4 strips, each ¾" x 40", for 1st and 3rd borders

From background, cut:
2 strips, each 2¾" x 40", for 2nd border

From floral print, cut:
3 strips, each 3¾" x 40", for outer border

From assorted fabrics used in the quilt, cut:
100 squares, each 1½" x 1½", for prairie points

From backing fabric, cut:
1 square, 25" x 25", for backing
1 rectangle, 6" x 22", for sleeve

From lightweight batting, cut:
1 square, 25" x 25"

*If using scraps or fat quarters for the light and dark sides of the blocks, cut enough strip lengths of light and dark fabrics to total the required number of strips shown above.

Directions

1. Follow the Basic Instructions for "Piecing the Log Cabin Blocks" on pages 11–13. Make 36 blocks as shown.

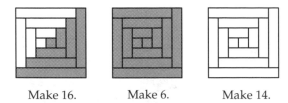

Make 16.   Make 6.   Make 14.

2. Arrange the blocks to form a heart as shown in the quilt plan on page 57. Sew the blocks together in horizontal rows. Press the seams of alternating rows in opposite directions.

3. Sew the rows together, making sure to match the seams between each block.

4. To add first border, measure the quilt through the center for the correct side border length as shown on page 16. Cut 2 black border strips to the correct length and sew to opposite sides of the quilt top. Measure the width of the quilt through the center, including the side borders. Cut 2 black border strips to the correct length and sew to the top and bottom edges of the quilt top.

5. It is much easier to appliqué the hearts, flowers, leaves, and stems onto the border before sewing the borders in place. Measure the quilt through the center for the correct side border length and cut two 2¾" background strips to the correct length.

6. Using the template patterns at right and one of the methods described on pages 13–14, prepare the appliqué pieces. For stems, iron paper-backed fusible web to wrong side of fabric for stems. Cut 2 strips, each a scant ¼" x 10" for side borders. Cut 2 strips, each a scant ¼" x 14½" for top and bottom borders

7. Center the 10" stems on the side borders and arrange the hearts, flowers, leaves, and stems as shown in the quilt plan on page 57. Press the design in place with a hot iron. Appliqué the design, following the directions for "Machine Appliqué" on pages 14–15. Sew the appliquéd side borders to each side of the quilt top.

8. Measure the width of the quilt through the center, including the side borders. Cut two 2¾" background strips to the correct width. Arrange the design on the top and bottom borders as shown in the quilt plan. Appliqué the hearts, flowers, leaves, and stems and attach the top and bottom borders to the quilt top.

9. Measure and add the third and outer borders as described in step 4 above.

10. Layer the quilt with batting and backing; pin baste, using safety pins.

11. Quilt around the Log Cabin heart design. Free-motion quilt around the hearts, flowers, and leaves. Quilt in-the-ditch around the remaining borders, ending with a row of quilting in the outer border, ½" from the third border. See page 18.

12. Follow the Basic Instructions for "Making Prairie Points" on pages 21–23 to finish the quilt.

13. Attach the sleeve to the back of the quilt. See page 19.

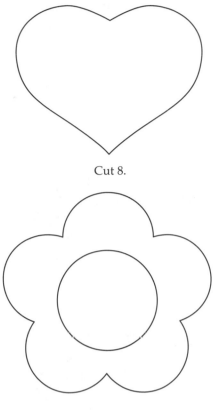

Cut 8.

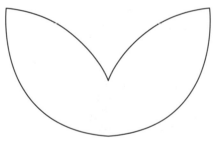

Cut 4 flowers
and 4 centers.

Cut 12.

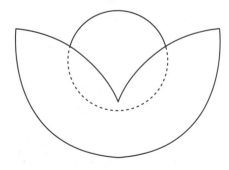

Cut 8 flowers
and 8 centers.

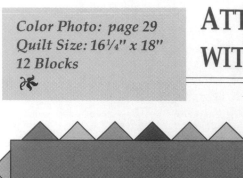

Color Photo: *page 29*
Quilt Size: 16¼" x 18"
12 Blocks

ATTIC WINDOWS
WITH APPLIQUÉ FLORAL BORDER

Quilt Plan

Cutting

Cut all strips across the fabric width (crosswise grain).

From assorted light fabrics*, cut a total of:
6 strips, each ¾" x 40"

From assorted dark fabrics*, cut a total of:
6 strips, each ¾" x 40"

From solid color, cut:
1 strip, ¾" x 10", for center of blocks

From black fabric, cut:
2 strips, each ¾" x 40", for 1st and 3rd borders

From background fabric, cut:
1 strip, 2 ¾" x 40", for 2nd border

From floral print, cut:
2 strips, each 3" x 40", for outer border

From assorted fabrics used in the quilt, cut:
72 squares, each 1½" x 1½", for prairie points

From backing fabric, cut:
1 rectangle, 18" x 20", for backing
1 rectangle, 6" x 15", for sleeve

From lightweight batting, cut:
1 rectangle, 18" x 20"

*If using scraps or fat quarters for the light and dark sides of the blocks, cut enough strip lengths of light and dark fabrics to total the required number of strips shown above.

Directions

Make 12.

1. Follow the Basic Instructions for "Piecing the Log Cabin Blocks" on pages 11–13. Make 12 blocks as shown.

2. Arrange the blocks in the Attic Window design as shown in the quilt plan on page 60. Sew the blocks together in horizontal rows. Press the seams of alternating rows in opposite directions.

3. Sew the rows together, making sure to match the seams between each block.

4. To add first border, measure the quilt through the center for the correct side border length as shown on page 16. Cut 2 black border strips to the correct length and sew to opposite sides of the quilt top. Measure the width of the quilt through the center, including the side

MATERIALS
44"-WIDE FABRIC

Use as many fabrics as possible in the colors of your choice for traditional Log Cabin blocks.

⅛ yd. each of 6 to 8 lights and 6 to 8 darks

⅛ yd. black for 1st and 3rd borders

⅛ yd. background for 2nd border

⅓ yd. floral print for outer border

⅝ yd. for backing and sleeve

Scrap of solid color for center of blocks

4 to 5 assorted greens for leaves, each 3" x 3"

6 or 7 assorted colors for flowers, each 3" x 4"

Yellow for flower centers, 3" x 3"

⅝ yd. lightweight batting

Note: Scraps of light and dark fabrics or fat quarters may also be used for the Log Cabin blocks.

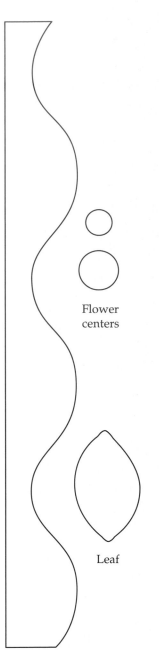

Flower centers

Leaf

Stem Template Guide

borders. Cut 2 black border strips to the correct length and sew to the top and bottom edges of the quilt top.

5. It is much easier to appliqué the flowers and leaves onto the border before sewing the borders in place. Measure the quilt through the center for the correct side border length and cut two 2¾" background strips to the correct length.

6. Using the template patterns at left and below and one of the methods described on pages 13–14, prepare the appliqué pieces.

7. Arrange the flowers and leaves on the side borders as shown in the quilt plan on page 60. Press the design in place with a hot iron. Appliqué the design, following the directions for "Machine Appliqué" on pages 14–15. Before removing the tear-away stabilizer, use a permanent fine-line brown or black pen to add stems and tendrils around the appliqué. Draw the stems free-hand, or use the Stem Template Guide at left. Sew the appliquéd side borders to each side of the quilt top.

8. Measure the width of the quilt through the center, including the side borders. Cut two 2¾" background strips to the correct width. Arrange the flowers and leaves on the top and bottom borders as shown in the quilt plan and appliqué. Before removing the tear-away stabilizer, use a permanent fine-line brown or black pen to add stems and tendrils around the appliqué. Sew the top and bottom borders to the quilt top.

9. Measure and add the third and outer borders as described in step 4.

10. Layer the quilt with batting and backing; pin baste, using safety pins.

11. Quilt around the Log Cabin blocks and borders. Free-motion quilt around the flowers and leaves. End with a row of quilting in the outer border, ½" from the third border. See page 18.

12. Follow the Basic Instructions for "Making Prairie Points" on pages 21–23 to finish the quilt.

13. Attach the sleeve to the back of the quilt. See page 19.

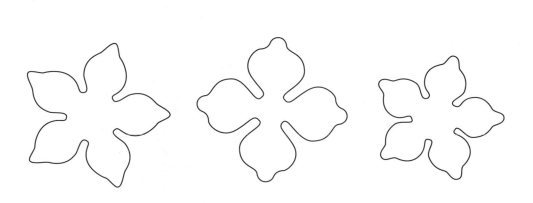

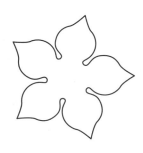

Cut:
12 Assorted flowers
6 Large flower centers
6 Small flower centers
24 Leaves

SANTAS IN THE FOREST

Color Photo: page 29
Quilt Size: 18½" x 21"
12 Log Cabin Blocks
6 Santa Blocks

Quilt Plan

MATERIALS
44"-WIDE FABRIC

Use as many fabrics as possible in the colors of your choice for traditional Log Cabin blocks.

⅛ yd. each of 6 to 8 lights and 6 to 8 darks

Scrap of solid color for center of blocks

⅛ yd. black for 1st and 3rd borders

⅓ yd. light background print for Santa blocks, corner triangles, side triangles, and 2nd border

½ yd. Christmas print for outer border

Red print for Santa's body, 3" x 12"

White for Santa's beard, 3" x 4"

Flesh or pink for Santa's face, 3" x 3"

Black for Santa's boots, 3" x 3"

Assorted reds for holly berries, each 3" x 3"

Assorted greens for holly leaves, each 4" x 5"

⅝ yd. for backing and sleeve

½ yd. lightweight batting

Note: Scraps of light and dark fabrics or fat quarters may also be used for the Log Cabin blocks.

Cutting

Cut all strips across the fabric width (crosswise grain).

From assorted light fabrics*, cut a total of:
6 strips, each ¾" x 40"

From assorted dark green fabrics*, cut a total of:
6 strips, each ¾" x 40"

From solid color, cut:
1 strip, ¾" x 10", for center of blocks

From black fabric, cut:
2 strips, each ¾" x 40", for 1st and 3rd borders

From background print, cut:
2 strips, each 2¾" x 40", for 2nd border

From Christmas print, cut:
3 strips, each 3" x 40", for outer border

From assorted prints used in the quilt, cut:
100 squares, each 1½" x 1½", for prairie points

From backing fabric, cut:
1 rectangle, 20" x 23", for backing
1 rectangle, 6" x 17", for sleeve

From lightweight batting, cut:
1 rectangle, 20" x 23"

*If using scraps or fat quarters for the light and dark sides of the blocks, cut enough strip lengths of light and dark fabrics to total the required number of strips shown above.

Directions

1. Follow the Basic Instructions for "Piecing the Log Cabin Blocks" on pages 11–13. Make 12 blocks as shown.

Make 12.

2. Using the template patterns on page 66, make plastic templates for the background square, corner, and side triangle.

3. It is important to match the size of the Log Cabin blocks and the background appliqué squares. Compare the completed Log Cabin blocks with the square template. You can either trim the edges of the

Log Cabin blocks to match the template, or trim the edges of the template to match the Log Cabin blocks.

4. Using the plastic templates, cut 6 squares, 4 corner triangles, and 10 side triangles from background fabric.

5. Using the template patterns on page 66 and one of the methods described on pages 13–14, prepare the appliqué pieces for the Santas, holly berries, and leaves.

6. Follow the Basic Instructions for "Machine Appliqué" on pages 14–15 to appliqué the Santas to the background squares.

7. Arrange the Log Cabin blocks, Santa blocks, and triangles as shown, remembering to turn the the dark side of the Log Cabin blocks up to resemble trees. The side triangles and corner triangles are larger than necessary. You will trim them before adding inner border. Sew the blocks in diagonal rows. Press the seams of alternating rows in opposite directions.

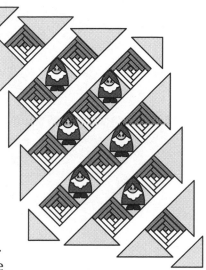

8. Sew the rows together, making sure to match the seams between each block. Add the corner triangles last.

9. Trim sides and square up corners. See step 9, page 45.

10. To add the first border, measure the quilt through the center for the correct side border length as shown on page 16. Cut 2 black border strips to the correct length and sew to opposite sides of the quilt top. Measure the width of the quilt through the center, including the side borders. Cut 2 black border strips to the correct length and sew to the top and bottom edges of the quilt top.

11. It is much easier to appliqué the holly leaves and berries to the border before sewing the borders in place. Measure the quilt through the center for the correct side border length and cut two 2¾" background strips to the correct length.

12. Arrange the holly berries and leaves on the side borders as shown in the quilt plan on page 63. Press the design in place with a hot iron. Appliqué the design, following the directions for "Machine Appliqué" on pages 14–15. Before removing the tear-away stabilizer, use a permanent fine-line brown or black pen to add stems and tendrils around the appliqué. Draw the stems free-hand, or use the Stem Template Guide on page 62. Sew the appliquéd side borders to each side of the quilt top.

13. Measure the width of the quilt through the center, including the side borders. Cut two 2¾" background strips to the correct width. Arrange the holly leaves and berries on the top and bottom borders as shown in the quilt plan and appliqué. Before removing the tear-away stabilizer, use a permanent fine-line brown or black pen to add stems

and tendrils around the appliqué. Attach the top and bottom borders to the quilt top.

14. Measure and add the third and outer borders as described in step 9.

15. Layer the quilt with batting and backing; pin baste, using safety pins.

16. Quilt around the Log Cabin blocks and borders, ending with a row of quilting in the outer border, ½" from the third border. Free-motion quilt around the Santas, holly berries, and leaves. See page 18.

17. Follow the Basic Instructions for "Making Prairie Points" on pages 21–23 to finish the quilt.

18. Attach the sleeve to the back of the quilt. See page 19.

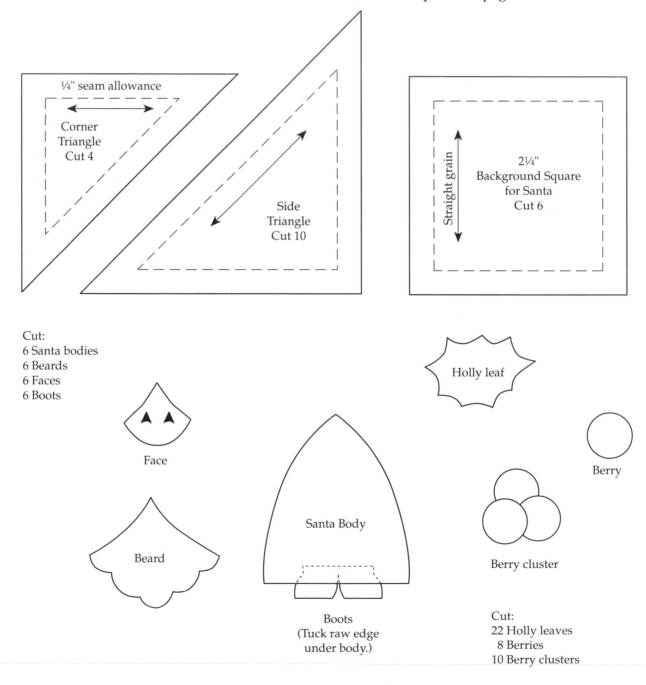

¼" seam allowance

Corner
Triangle
Cut 4

Side
Triangle
Cut 10

Straight grain

2¼"
Background Square
for Santa
Cut 6

Cut:
6 Santa bodies
6 Beards
6 Faces
6 Boots

Holly leaf

Face

Berry

Beard

Santa Body

Berry cluster

Boots
(Tuck raw edge
under body.)

Cut:
22 Holly leaves
8 Berries
10 Berry clusters

LIVELY BARN RAISING

Color Photo: page 30
Quilt Size: 20½" x 20½"
36 Blocks

Quilt Plan

MATERIALS
44"-WIDE FABRIC

Use as many fabrics as possible in the colors of your choice for traditional Log Cabin blocks.

⅛ yd. each of 6 to 8 lights and 6 to 8 darks

⅛ yd. solid color for center of blocks

⅛ yd. black for 1st and 3rd borders

⅛ yd. contrasting fabric for 2nd border

⅓ yd. floral print for outer border and binding

⅝ yd. for backing and sleeve

⅝ yd. lightweight batting

Note: Scraps of light and dark fabrics or fat quarters may also be used for the Log Cabin blocks.

Cutting

Cut all strips across the fabric width (crosswise grain).

From assorted light fabrics*, cut a total of:
   10 strips, each ¾" x 40"

From assorted dark fabrics*, cut a total of:
   10 strips, each ¾" x 40"

From solid color, cut:
   1 strip, ¾" x 40", for center of blocks

From black fabric, cut:
   4 strips, each ¾" x 40", for 1st and 3rd borders

From contrasting fabric, cut:
   2 strips, each 1¾" x 40", for 2nd border

From floral print, cut:
   2 strips, each 3½" x 40", for outer border
   3 strips, each 1¾" x 40", for binding

From backing fabric, cut:
   1 square, 22" x 22", for backing
   1 rectangle, 6" x 19", for sleeve

From lightweight batting, cut:
   1 square, 22" x 22"

*If using scraps or fat quarters for the light and dark sides of the blocks, cut enough strip lengths of light and dark fabrics to total the required number of strips shown above.

Directions

1. Follow the Basic Instructions for "Piecing the Log Cabin Blocks" on pages 11–13. Make 36 blocks as shown.

2. Arrange the blocks to form the Barn Raising design as shown in the quilt plan on page 67. Sew the blocks together in horizontal rows. Press the seams of alternating rows in opposite directions.

3. Sew the rows together, making sure to match the seams between each block.

4. To add the first border, measure the quilt through the center for the correct side border length as shown on page 16. Cut 2 black border

strips to the correct length and sew to opposite sides of the quilt top. Measure the width of the quilt through the center, including the side borders. Cut 2 black border strips to the correct length and sew to the top and bottom edges of the quilt top.

5. Measure and add the second, third, and outer borders as described in step 4.

6. Layer the quilt with batting and backing; pin baste, using safety pins.

7. Quilt around the Barn Raising design and in-the-ditch around all of the borders. Add one row of quilting in the outer border, ½" from the third border. See page 18.

8. Attach the sleeve and bind the edges of the quilt. See pages 19–21.

Accessories

These small projects make quick gifts for your quilting friends and are a great way to use up that leftover fabric.

Color Photo: page 30
Small Pincushion:
1¾" x 1¾"
1 Block

Large Pincushion:
3½" x 3½"
4 Blocks

PINCUSHIONS

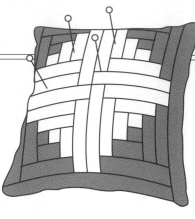

MATERIALS
44"-WIDE FABRIC

Scraps of assorted light and dark fabrics

Scraps of solid color for center of blocks

Backing fabric, either 2¼" x 2¼", or 4" x 4"

Interfacing, either 2¼" x 2¼", or 4" x 4"

Polyester fiberfill

Cutting

From assorted light and dark fabrics, cut:
Enough ¾"-wide strips to make either 1 or 4 Log Cabin blocks, depending on the size pincushion you are making.

Directions

1. Follow the Basic Instructions for "Piecing the Log Cabin Blocks" on pages 11–13. Make 1 or 4 blocks.

2. Sew the blocks together in one of the arrangements shown.

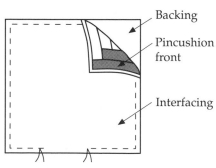

Backing

Pincushion front

Interfacing

3. Cut a square of interfacing and a square of backing fabric the same size as the pincushion. Place the interfacing on the wrong side of the pincushion top, then place the back on the pincushion top with right sides together. Sew all three pieces together, using a ¼"-wide seam allowance, leaving an opening on one side for turning.

4. Trim the corners, turn right side out, and press.

5. Firmly stuff pincushion with fiberfill, making sure the fiberfill is between the interfacing and the back of the pincushion. Blindstitch the opening closed.

ORNAMENTS AND KEY CHAINS

Color Photo: page 30
Size: 2¼" x 2¼"
1 Block

Ornament

Key ring

Cutting

From assorted light and dark fabrics, cut:
Enough ¾"-wide strips to make as many Log Cabin blocks for as many ornaments or key chains you intend to make

From solid color, cut:
1 strip, ¾" wide and long enough for the centers of all your blocks

MATERIALS
44"-WIDE FABRIC

Scraps of assorted light and dark fabrics

Scraps of solid color for center of blocks

Backing fabric, 4" x 4"

Lightweight batting, 4" x 4"

Brass ring for each key chain

3" length of ⅛"-wide ribbon for each key chain

20" length of 1/16"- or ⅛"-wide ribbon for each ornament

Optional: small bell for each ornament

Directions

1. Follow the Basic Instructions for "Piecing the Log Cabin Blocks" on pages 11–13. Make the number of blocks desired.

2. From backing fabric, cut a square 1" larger than the block. From lightweight batting, cut a square the same size as the block. Layer the block, batting, and backing together to make a quilt sandwich. Using metallic thread and a decorative stitch, machine quilt in the block.

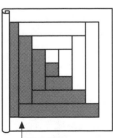

Backing

3. Fold ¼" of the backing fabric over to the front, then fold ¼" again to the top of the block. Machine stitch, using a blind hem stitch, or blindstitch by hand. This technique takes the place of binding.

4. *For ornament:* Tie a bow in the ribbon, leaving a 3" loop for hanging. Tack to one corner of the ornament. If desired, sew a small bell to the opposite corner of the ornament.

5. *For key chain:* Cut a 3" length of ⅛"-wide ribbon. Fold the ribbon in half and insert through a brass key ring. Tuck the ends of the ribbon into one folded corner of the block before it is stitched. Finish stitching and secure ends in place.

Tip

Save pieces of batting from larger quilting projects to use in these smaller projects.

Color Photo: page 31
Size: 4" x 7¾"
3 Blocks

CHECKBOOK COVER

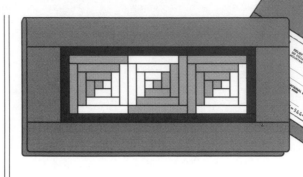

MATERIALS
44"-WIDE FABRIC

⅓ yd. floral print for checkbook cover

Scraps of assorted light and dark fabrics

Scraps of solid color for center of blocks

Scraps of black for inner border

Heavyweight interfacing or a tear-away type stabilizer for stiffening (not to be torn away), 3" x 16"

Lightweight batting or fleece, 9" x 9"

Cutting

From assorted light and dark fabrics, cut:
Enough ¾"-wide strips to make 3 Log Cabin blocks

From solid color, cut:
1 strip, ¾" x 3", for center of blocks

Directions

1. Follow the Basic Instructions for "Piecing the Log Cabin Blocks" on pages 11–13. Make 3 blocks.

2. Sew the blocks together horizontally for the front of the checkbook cover.

3. To add inner border, measure the short ends of the row of blocks. Cut 2 black border strips, ¾" x the length, and sew to opposite ends. Measure the long sides of the row of blocks including the side borders. Cut 2 black border strips, ¾" x the length, and sew to the top and bottom of the blocks.

4. Measure and cut 1¼"-wide floral print border strips for outer border; attach as described in step 3 above.

5. From the floral print, cut a rectangle for the back, the same size as the checkbook cover front. With right sides together, sew the checkbook front to the back along one long edge, using a ¼"-wide seam allowance. Press the front and back open.

6. From the floral print, cut a rectangle for the lining the same size as the checkbook front and back. Layer the checkbook top, batting, and lining to make a quilt sandwich. Machine quilt around the

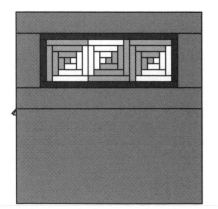

Log Cabin blocks and quilt 3 rows of stitching approximately 1¼"
apart on the back of the checkbook cover as shown.

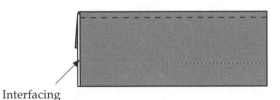

Approx.
1¼"

7. *To make the pockets:* Measure the width of the checkbook. Cut 2
   rectangles from the interfacing, each 3" x the width of the checkbook cover. Cut 2 rectangles from the floral print, each 4½" x the
   width.

8. Place the interfacing on the wrong side of the pocket rectangles,
   matching the long edges. Fold the opposite side of the fabric over
   the interfacing and press in place. Topstitch ¼" from the folded
   edge with a straight or decorative stitch. Make 2 pockets.

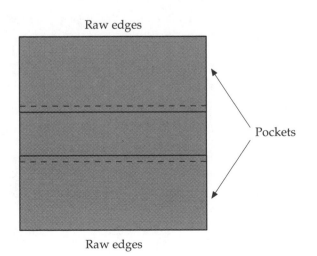

Interfacing

9. Matching raw edges, place one pocket on the inside front, and the
   other pocket on the inside back. Pin in place until binding is
   added.

Raw edges

Pockets

Raw edges

10. Follow the Basic Instructions for "Binding" on pages 20–21 to bind
    checkbook cover.

Size: 4¼" x 4¼"
Color Photo: page 31
1 Block

NEEDLE CASE

MATERIALS
44"-WIDE FABRIC

¼ yd. floral print for needle case

Scraps of assorted light and dark fabrics

Scraps of solid color for center of block

Scraps of black for inner border

Felt or fleece to make heart to hold pins, 3" x 3"

Lightweight batting, 5" x 9"

Heavyweight interfacing or tear-away stabilizer for stiffening (not to be torn away), 4" x 9"

12" of ⅛"- or ¹⁄₁₆"-wide ribbon for bow

Brass charm for embellishment (optional)

1 nylon snap

Cutting

From assorted light and dark fabrics, cut:
Enough ¾"-wide strips to make 1 Log Cabin block

Directions

1. Follow the Basic Instructions for "Piecing the Log Cabin Blocks" on pages 11–13. Make 1 block.

2. To add inner border, measure the block. Cut 2 black border strips, ¾" x the length, and sew to opposite sides of the block. Measure the width of the block, including the side borders. Cut 2 black border strips, ¾" x the length, and sew to the top and bottom of the block.

3. Measure and cut 1¼"-wide floral print border strips for outer border; attach as described in step 2 above.

4. From the floral print, cut a square for the back the same size as the needle case front. With right sides facing, place needle case front and back together. Sew along one side, using a ¼"-wide seam allowance. Press the front and back open.

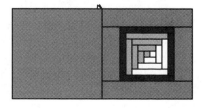

5. From the floral print, cut a rectangle for the lining, 1" larger than the size of the needle case front and back. Layer the needle case top, batting, and lining to make a quilt sandwich.

6. Using a straight or decorative stitch, machine quilt around the Log Cabin block with metallic or monofilament thread. Then add 2 lines of quilting on the back, approximately 1½" apart, as shown.

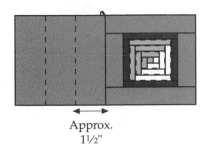

Approx.
1½"

7. *To make the pocket:* Measure the length of the needle case front and back. From the interfacing, cut 1 rectangle, 3½" x the length. From the floral print, cut 1 rectangle, 4¼" x the length. Place interfacing on wrong side of floral print rectangle, matching the long edges. Fold the opposite end of the fabric over the interfacing and press. Topstitch ¼" from the folded edge, using a decorative stitch if desired.

8. *To add felt heart:* Make a plastic template of the heart pattern below. Cut out 1 heart from felt or fleece. Fold the pocket in half with right sides facing and the stitched edge at the top. Pin the felt heart to the center of the right side. Follow the Basic Instructions for "Machine Appliqué" on pages 14–15 to appliqué the heart in place.

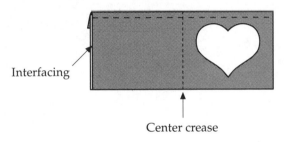

Interfacing

Center crease

9. Matching lower raw edges, place pocket on inside of needle case. Stitch pocket to needle case along center crease line.

10. Follow the Basic Instructions for "Binding" on pages 20–21 to bind edges of needle case.

11. To finish, sew a nylon snap on inside center edges; if desired, add a bow and brass charm to one corner of the Log Cabin block.

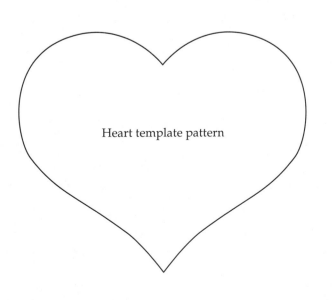

Heart template pattern

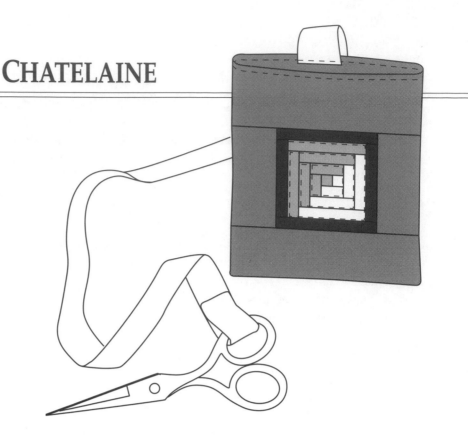

Color Photo: page 32
Size: 3¾" x 4¼"

CHATELAINE

MATERIALS
44"-WIDE FABRIC

¼ yd. floral print for chatelaine and lining

Scraps of assorted light and dark fabrics

Scrap of solid color for center of block

Scraps of black for inner border

Lightweight batting, 4" x 8"

1 yd. ⅝"-wide grosgrain ribbon

Loop and hook fastener, such as Velcro, for scissor loop

⅓ yd. of ¹⁄₁₆"- or ⅛"-wide ribbon for bow (optional)

Brass charm for embellishment (optional)

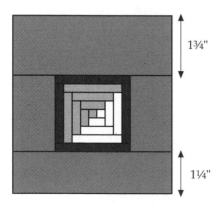

Cutting

From assorted light and dark fabrics, cut:
Enough ¾"-wide strips to make 1 Log Cabin block

Directions

1. Follow the Basic Instructions for "Piecing the Log Cabin Blocks" on pages 11–13. Make 1 block.

2. To add inner border, measure the block. Cut 2 black border strips, ¾" x the length, and sew to opposite sides of the block. Measure the width of the block, including the side borders. Cut 2 black border strips, ¾" x the length, and sew to the top and bottom of the block.

3. Measure and cut three 1¼"-wide floral print border strips for outer border; attach to opposite sides and bottom of block. Measure and cut a 1¾"-wide floral print border strip for remaining side (top); sew to top of block.

4. From the floral print, cut a rectangle for the back the same size as the chatelaine front. Place chatelaine front and back together, with right sides facing. Sew together along the bottom edge, using a ¼"-wide seam allowance. Press front and back open.

5. Cut a rectangle of batting the same size as the chatelaine front and back. Place the batting on the wrong side of the chatelaine. Using a straight or decorative stitch, machine quilt around the Log Cabin block with metallic or monofilament thread. Then add 2 lines of quilting on the back as shown.

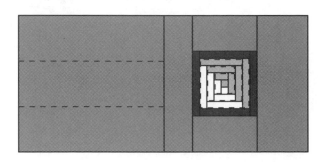

6. Cut a rectangle for the lining, ½" shorter than the length of the chatelaine front and back. Place the chatelaine top and the lining together, with right sides facing. Sew along both narrow edges, using a ¼"-wide seam allowance.

7. Fold the entire unit so that seams that were sewn in step 6 meet in the middle. Sew a ¼"-wide seam around raw edges, leaving a 3" opening on one edge of the lining for turning.

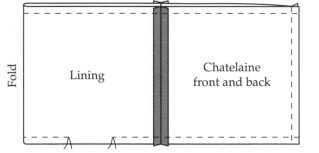

Fold

Lining

Chatelaine front and back

8. Turn inside out. Fold raw edges of opening toward the inside and stitch opening closed with a ¹⁄₁₆"-wide seam. Tuck lining inside case. Topstitch around the opening.

9. Sew one end of the grosgrain ribbon to the inside back center of the pocket. On the other end of the ribbon, fold end of ribbon over ½" and stitch one piece of hook and one piece of loop Velcro, about 1" apart, to hold scissors.

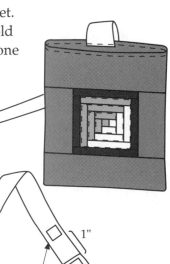

1"

Velcro

Tip

Try using a hemostat for turning small projects right side out. These can often be found in drugstores.

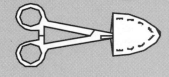

10. Sew a nylon snap inside the top center of the chatelaine to close.

Color Photo: page 31
Size: 3" x 6 ¼"
❧

MATERIALS
44"-WIDE FABRIC

⅛ yd. floral print for eyeglass case and lining

Scraps of assorted light and dark fabrics

Scrap of solid color for center of blocks

Scraps of black for inner border

Lightweight batting, 4" x 14"

EYEGLASS CASE

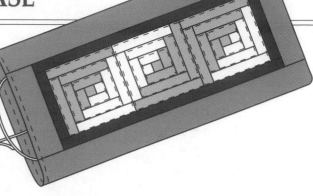

Cutting

From assorted light and dark fabrics, cut:
Enough ¾"-wide strips to make 3 Log Cabin blocks

Directions

1. Follow the Basic Instructions for "Piecing the Log Cabin Blocks" on pages 11–13. Make 3 blocks.

2. Sew the blocks together horizontally for the front of the eyeglass case.

3. To add inner border, measure the short ends of the row of blocks. Cut 2 black border strips, ¾" x the length, and sew to the short ends. Measure the long sides of the row of blocks including the side borders. Cut 2 black border strips, ¾" x the length, and sew to the long sides of the blocks.

4. Measure and cut 1"-wide floral print border strips for outer border; attach as described in step 3 above.

5. From the floral print, cut a rectangle for the back, the same size as the front. Place eyeglass front and back together, with right sides facing. Sew together along one short end, using a ¼"-wide seam allowance. Press the front and back open.

6. Cut a rectangle of batting the same size as the front and back of the eyeglass case. Using a straight or decorative stitch, machine quilt around the Log Cabin blocks with metallic or monofilament thread. Then add 2 lines of quilting on the back, approximately 1¼" apart, as shown.

Approx. 1¼"

7. For the lining, cut a rectangle ½" shorter than the length of the eyeglass case front and back. Place the eyeglass case top and the lining together, with right sides facing. Sew along both narrow edges, using a ¼"-wide seam allowance.

8. Fold the entire unit so that seams that were sewn in step 7 meet in the middle. Sew a ¼"-wide seam around raw edges, leaving a 3" opening on one edge of the lining for turning.

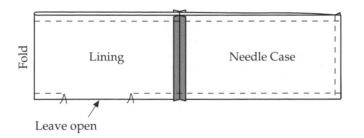

Leave open

9. Turn inside out. Fold raw edges of opening toward the inside and stitch opening closed with a ¹⁄₁₆"-wide seam. Tuck lining inside case. Topstitch around the opening.

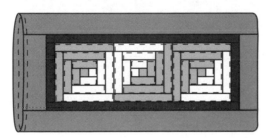

Color Photo: page 32
Size: 4" x 4"

NAME TAG

MATERIALS
44"-WIDE FABRIC

Scraps of assorted light and dark fabrics

Scraps of solid color for center of blocks

Muslin, 3" x 3"

Floral print for backing, 4" x 4"

Scraps of contrasting fabric for binding

Lightweight batting, 4" x 4"

Safety pin

Cutting

From assorted light and dark fabrics, cut:
Enough ¾"-wide strips to make 4 Log Cabin blocks

Directions

1. Follow the Basic Instructions for "Piecing the Log Cabin Blocks" on pages 11–13. Make 4 blocks.

2. Sew the blocks together in one of the arrangements shown.

3. Make a plastic template of one of the heart patterns on page 24.

4. Iron a piece of paper-backed fusible web to the back of a piece of muslin. Do not peel the paper away until after you have drawn or written on the muslin. It helps to stabilize the fabric.

5. Using a light box if necessary, trace the heart and one of the designs onto the muslin with a permanent pen, or be creative and draw your own design; add the name.

6. Cut out the heart. Remove the paper; place in the center of the block and press with a hot iron.

7. Following the Basic Instructions for "Machine Appliqué" on pages 13–15, appliqué the heart in place, using a decorative stitch and metallic thread or a complementary color of cotton embroidery thread. Leave the tear-away stabilizer in place for stability.

8. Cut a square of batting and backing the same size as the name tag. Layer the name-tag top, batting, and backing to make a quilt sandwich.

9. Outline quilt around the heart and between the 4 blocks.

10. Following the Basic Instructions for "Binding" on pages 20–21, bind the edges of the name tag.

11. Sew a safety pin at the top of the back, so you can wear your name tag proudly.